The Best Cartoons from
Leadership
Journal

Volume 4

The Best Cartoons from
Leadership *Journal*

Volume 4

BROADMAN
& HOLMAN
PUBLISHERS

Nashville, Tennessee

Published by Broadman & Holman Publishers,
Nashville, Tennessee
Editorial Team: Leonard G. Goss, John Landers, Sandra Bryer

0-8054-1295-6

Dewey Decimal Classification: 817
Subject Heading: HUMOR

You may reprint LEADERSHIP cartoons under the following guidelines:
1. The reprints are used in the ministry of your church or classroom.
2. The prepared materials are distributed without cost.
3. Fewer than 1,000 copies will be printed
4. The following credit line appears on the first page of each copy:
   "Copyright 1999 from Christianity Today, Inc. Used with permission."
If more than 1,000 copies of the material are to be printed, permission must then be requested from the individual author/cartoonist. Addresses and phone numbers are available upon request from Christianity Today, Inc., 465 Gundersen Drive, Carol Stream, IL 60188-2498.

01 02 03 04 05 03 02 01 00 99

"Look at me. I've gone into the ministry!"

© 1998 Lee Johnson

"Oh great and powerful Oz, Toto and I want to return home, the Scarecrow wants a brain, the Tin Man wants a heart, the Lion wants courage, and the Pastor wants a stable church in a small town with a supportive but not smothering congregation."

Murphy's Multiple Staff
Tom is in charge of setting the vision,
Dick is in charge of counseling,
and Harry handles most of the pulpit duties.

"Believe me, fellows, everyone from the Pharaoh on down
is an equally valued member of the team."

MEET
YOUR
CHURCH
STAFF

© 1995 Dik LaPine

"What do you mean...reluctance to accept your leadership? That's ridiculous, Pastor."

"Are you questioning my authority again,
Mrs. Thundermuffin?"

"According to a new religious journal, this is how much power we actually have."

New pastor Leo Oxnard wasted no time establishing
himself as leader of the board.

"I heard you like your associates to speak their mind.
Is that true, Melon-Head?"

11

Staff relations begin to show signs of strain.

© 1996 Steve Phelps

"Nobody move!"

"I want you all to remember that we are a team."

"Advise me, yes—contradict me, no!"

16

"So I say to my new associate, 'Be your own man.
Don't be like everyone else.'"

17

© 1985 Erik Johnson

"I see your pastor hand-picks his leaders."

19

The Ideal Pastor

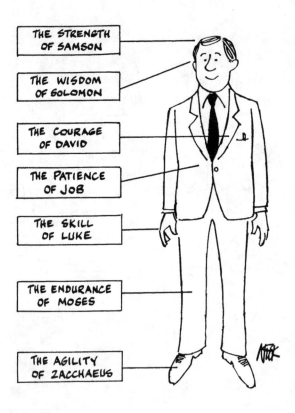

THE STRENGTH OF SAMSON

THE WISDOM OF SOLOMON

THE COURAGE OF DAVID

THE PATIENCE OF JOB

THE SKILL OF LUKE

THE ENDURANCE OF MOSES

THE AGILITY OF ZACCHAEUS

© 1984 Nick Hobart

21

The Weekly Evolution of a Pastor

Sunday   Monday   Tuesday

© 1990 David McGinnis

22

Wednesday   **Thursday**   **Friday**   **Saturday**

"Say hello to the Reverend Martin Green,
the Very Reverend Andrew Crowe, and the
Mega-Reverend Stephen Knowles."

"He was traded to Valley Church for a music
director and a youth pastor."

"Just between you and me, Pastor, what's a nice guy like you doin' in a job like this?"

"You're the former pastor?"

"Give me the Bill Hybels look."

Visiting the museum, Pastor Harrows
realizes that he needs a new suit.

29

"Pastor always wanted to do that before he retired."

"There's a visitor here to see the 'Big Cheese.'"

"Today I'd like to share some impressions from my recent trip to Washington, D.C."

"It comes as a total surprise to be asked
to address the synod like this..."

The ministers' gathering was going well until the
question came up, "How's your church doing?"

"We're in debt, the deacons have all quit, and we've not had a visitor in six months. But thank goodness none of the other churches are doing any better."

"Attendance is down!"

"The church bus needs a new engine!"

"We're barely paying our bills!"

"Pastor Lewis, speaking."

© 1981 Rob Portlock

"I don't think this is what Professor Smith meant about becoming an effective change agent."

© 1980 LEADERSHIP. Art: Rolland Dingman

"I'm sorry, Brother Markley, but I'm already
fast-forwarding as fast as I can."

"I'm not sure giving Pastor that book on Strengthening Your Grip was such a good idea."

WHERE THE BEATLES GOT THEIR BEST STUFF

IT'S A CLOSELY GUARDED SECRET THAT THE INSPIRATION FOR MANY OF JOHN LENNON AND PAUL MCCARTNEY'S CLASSIC HITS CAME FROM MINISTERS!

THERE'S GOT TO BE SOME TROUBLE-FREE CHURCH OUT THERE THAT NEEDS ME...

FOOL ON THE HILL

WHERE THE BEATLES GOT THEIR BEST STUFF...

© 1994 Erik Johnson

Let It Beep

WHERE THE BEATLES GOT THEIR BEST STUFF...

© 1994 Erik Johnson

Pastor Pepper's Lonely Hearts Club Recovery Group

Penny Lane

WHERE THE BEATLES GOT THEIR BEST STUFF...

When I'm Sixty-Four

"Rev. Peterson is in the Holy Land, the youth pastor's under the church bus, and the minister of music is in jail for photocopying music. Want to talk to the janitor?"

"I guess my first question is,
Do you ever press charges?"

"What I like about him is he never tells you to stay in line, he asks you to stay in line."

"You've got to admire him. He's always quick to leave the ninety-nine to search for the lost one."

50

"While you were out, Constantine converted to Christianity, Luther spearheaded the Reformation, Wesleyan revivals broke out in England, Bryan won the Scopes trial, religious broadcasting swept the nation…"

51

"Hello there. Pastor Johnson is tied up
right now, but when you hear the bell,
you'll have 30 seconds to leave your message."

© 1981 LEADERSHIP. Art: Brenda Burbank

"Oh, I'm sure he won't mind our interrupting his hectic
schedule to chat for a while....Well that's funny,
he was here a minute ago!"

© 1992 Jerry Cogan

"Perhaps we shouldn't disturb him.
He seems to be deep in thought."

"Helen, be sure to remind me of
'National Secretary's Week.'"

"No, she can't type, but she really guards my study time."

© 1986 Artemas Cole

57

Eventually, of course, the abandoned warehouse
was discovered, and the town's ministers had to
find a new hide-out for their day off.

"You overscheduled again."

"So I had a couple hours with nuthin' to do, so I thought I'd drop in and see you..."

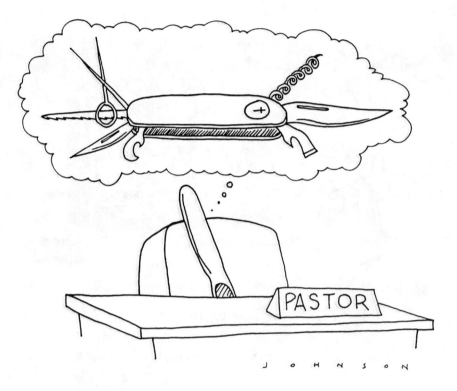

PASTOR

JOHNSON

"Sorry, the pastor won't be able to see you today.
He has paralysis of analysis."

"Come see the marvelous Pastor Bill!
Hear his sermons... Watch him organize and run
committees... Gasp as he repairs and maintains
the church singlehandedly... Observe him..."

64

He keeps going and going and going...

Midway through a hectic day, Pastor Reimer
realizes it was his day off.

© 1993 Penn Clark

"Excuse me, Pastor. Got a minute, or are you busy?"

The pastor's nightmare.

"Pastor Lewis has a new time-management system."

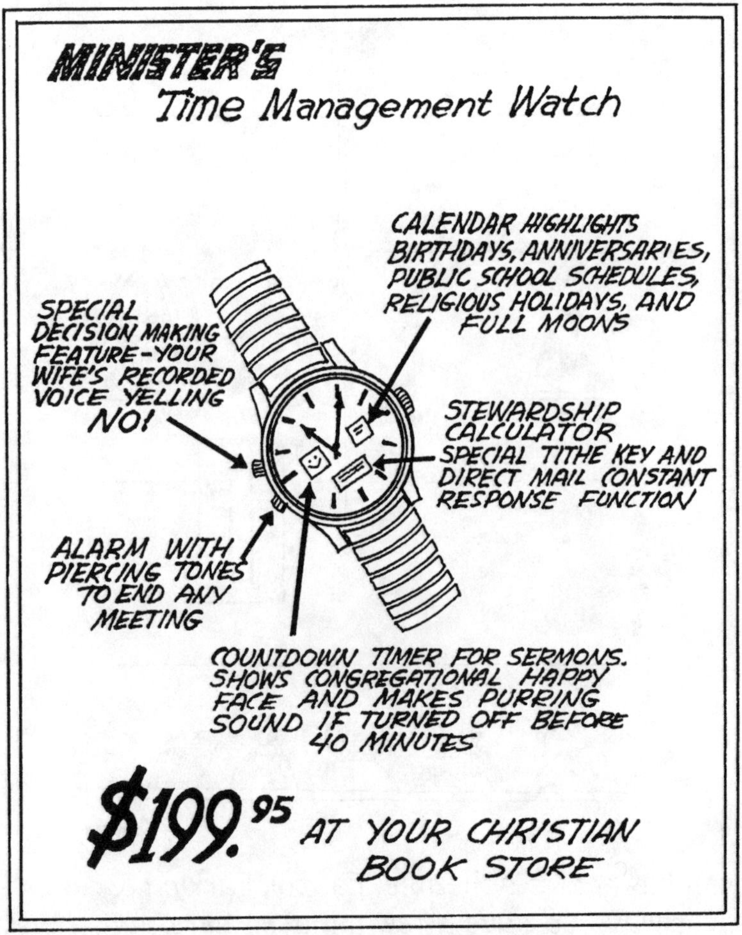
MINISTER'S
Time Management Watch
CALENDAR HIGHLIGHTS BIRTHDAYS, ANNIVERSARIES, PUBLIC SCHOOL SCHEDULES, RELIGIOUS HOLIDAYS, AND FULL MOONS
SPECIAL DECISION MAKING FEATURE-YOUR WIFE'S RECORDED VOICE YELLING NO!
STEWARDSHIP CALCULATOR SPECIAL TITHE KEY AND DIRECT MAIL CONSTANT RESPONSE FUNCTION
ALARM WITH PIERCING TONES TO END ANY MEETING
COUNTDOWN TIMER FOR SERMONS. SHOWS CONGREGATIONAL HAPPY FACE AND MAKES PURRING SOUND IF TURNED OFF BEFORE 40 MINUTES
$199.95 AT YOUR CHRISTIAN BOOK STORE

Given his hectic schedule, Pastor Farkle began looking
for ways to save a few minutes here and there.

God's Daytimer.

74

"I've decided to return to organized religion.
I cleaned my desk."

© 1987 Ed Koehler

76

INPUT OUTPUT PUT PUT

LIEBE

78

79

© 1988 Artemas Cole

80

81

82

"And now for the privilege of telling the custodian about the all-night-junior high water-balloon and caramel-corn party."

"Pastor's a genius at selecting
the right people for the right jobs."

85

Pastoral Paralysis

87

The Pastor's Feet: As Seen By...

...His Wife

...His Teenage Children

...His Congregation

...Himself

D.P.

"No, Ma'am, I'm not a preacher.
I've just been ill for a few days."

"And never, ever look at serving
the church as burdensome."

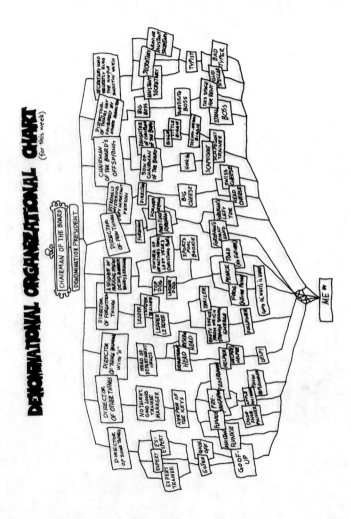

© 1983 LEADERSHIP

And on the 7th day...
Thou shalt attend the
men's breakfast, teach
Sunday School, preach two
sermons, chair a building
committee meeting, make
hospital rounds... and rest.

© 1989 Andy Robertson

92

"It was awesome, Pastor Bob! Right after you left, y'know, everybody else on staff came down with this really gnarly kind of flu. So, anyway, that left me to emcee the Crenshaw funeral last Saturday... Pastor Bob?"

© 1984 Doug Hall

"Ever have one of those days when you felt
you just had to rebuke someone?"

DISCOVERING THAT THE LIGHT AT THE END OF THE TUNNEL IS NEW JERSEY

© 1985 Nick Hobart

...you have no plans for the weekend, and your youth director asks if you would pleeease fill in for an absentee chaperone at the lock-in.

© 1990 Andy Robertson

...you're asked about your little "get-away"
that was actually a candidating trip.

IT'S HARD TO BE HONEST WHEN...

...you're twenty minutes late, and you wife asks, "How does my hair look, Honey?"

...Delbert Fleeble asks if you've read his poems
he gave you three months ago.

101

It was safe to say that Pastor Mel's
vision statement hadn't yet caught fire.

"That settles it. Our new vision statement will be:
MISERY LOVES COMPANY."

"I like to think of myself as the facilitator and enabler of this church rather than the senior pastor or chief executive officer."

"Now, Reverend Walden, do you still want to
do away with Sunday night services?"

"I don't think the pastor's going to change his mind on this subject."

"The pastor can sure paint a rosy picture."

"Well, what kind of job did he give you?"

"I'd like to answer charges that I'm inaccessible."

PASTORING IN THE '50s

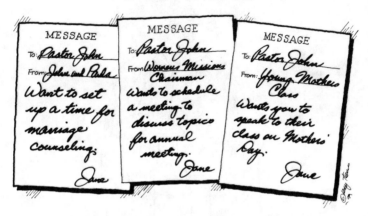

PASTORING IN THE '90s

"I like a pastor who makes things happen!"

Pastor Potts had never been late to church in 32 years, but when they began the early service, it was a bit of an adjustment.

"The board wants to know if this is coming off your conference time or your vacation."

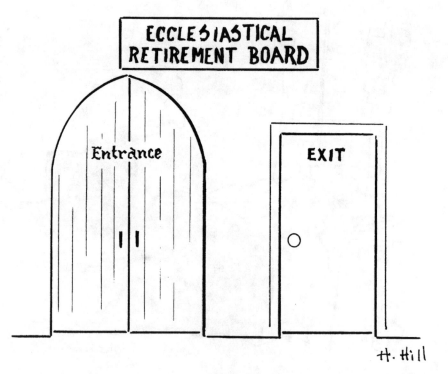

Job Security

116

OFFICE
PASTOR
ROBERT TYLER

117

"Remember back when we were young,
and the difference between clergy and laity
was none of the clergy were women?"

"I see you've had assistant pastor experience before."

"Actually, Martin, I prefer the term 'Assistant Pastor.'"

"I've done it!! I've created the perfect assistant pastor."

"Ladies and gentlemen, he's worked here
in obscurity for five years. Now, for the first time
on stage, our associate pastor!"

"I bet the assistant pastor will be glad
when his apprenticeship is over!"

"I heard it through the grapevine that
you need a minister of music."

"We're looking for someone with a doctorate in Christian education and five years of experience, but we'll settle for someone with a van."

"I assure you I'd make a fine director of Christian education. I've held that position in several previous lives."

© 1992 Ed Koehler

"We have opened new works in Bangladesh, Nepal, and Sri Lanka. How come we can't open the C.E. file cabinet?"

Pastor Dan begins to consider seriously the suggestion to hire a youth director.

© 1988 Steve Phelps

128

"I see our pastor and youth director are
in a staff meeting."

"Gee, Dad, you look great! The youth ministry
sure seems to agree with you!"

"You'll be responsible for developing spiritual maturity among our young people, who are the future of this church. We also need you to drive the van."

© 1994 Nick Hobart

"Okay, let's all stand, turn to our neighbors, and tell them if we wear boxers or tight whites."

The new youth director gets his first lesson
in "ownership of ideas."

"Guess what, Jim? I got a new set of commentaries for our pastor."

"Sounds like you made a pretty good trade."

"We could have been a bit hasty in putting
Schwartz in charge of the ushers."

© 1993 Erik Johnson

138

Pastor Earl's Monday Morning Ritual

"The worst case of pastor burnout I've ever seen."

"You know, maybe Reverend Hall is about due for a sabbatical."

A sure sign you're ready for a vacation.

"No, no, Jimmy. Grandpa is an interim pastor,
not a scab."

© 1997 Dan Pegoda

145

"Yes, we are looking for a new pastor, but we accept résumés only in the standard 8-by-11 format."

Another way to tell the previous
pastor had some problems.

"Ever notice how the eyes seem to
follow you around the room?"

New pastor Ralph Mumford
had his work cut out for him.

"Our previous pastor could do a triple axel."

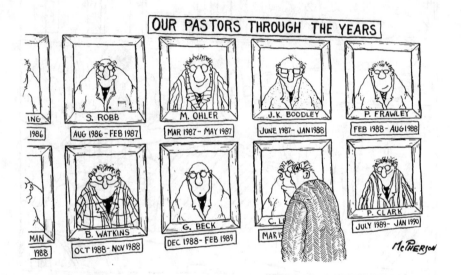

New Pastor Milton Feldspar began to wonder
what he'd gotten himself into.

"I still think he could do more for the church."

Tomb of the Unknown Pastor

Giving credit where credit is due.